D0503222

Meerkats

James Maclaine
Illustrated by Jeremy Norton

Additional illustrations by Roger Simó
Designed by Amy Manning

Meerkat consultant: Professor David Macdonald CBE
Wildlife Conservation Research Unit, Zoology Department, University of Oxford
Reading consultant: Alison Kelly

Contents

Curious creatures

Meerkats live in dry, sandy places in the south of Africa.

They have slender bodies and long tails.

A meerkat uses its tail to keep itself steady.

Furry bodies

Meerkats have pale brown fur. They try to keep it clean.

This meerkat is using its teeth to remove insects and dirt from another meerkat's fur.

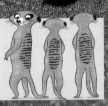

Every meerkat has its own pattern of stripes across its back.

Meerkats' tummies aren't very furry.

A meerkat warms the skin on its tummy in the sun.

If it gets too hot, the meerkat lies on a rock to cool down.

There are dark patches of fur around a meerkat's eyes.

They help it to see in bright sunlight.

Living together

Meerkats live in groups called mobs.
There can be up to 50 meerkats in a mob.

The meerkats in a
mob are different
ages and sizes.

A big female
meerkat and a big
male lead the mob.

These meerkats are from the same mob. They're huddling together to keep warm.

Burrow homes

Meerkats live in burrows under the ground, where they hide during the day and sleep at night.

These meerkats are peeking out from their burrow.

A burrow has lots of tunnels.

There are
several
ways in...

...and out...

Inside, there are
places where
meerkats rest.

Deep parts of the
burrow stay warm
when it's too hot or
cold above ground.

Some meerkats share their burrows with
yellow mongooses or ground squirrels.

Hungry diggers

Every day meerkats leave their burrows to find food. They search for insects, small animals and plants.

This meerkat is using its sharp claws to dig for things to eat.

Meerkats sniff the air and ground for smells when they hunt.

A meerkat smells a lizard that's hiding in the sand.

It quickly digs down to find the lizard before it escapes.

The meerkat catches the lizard with its paws and teeth.

Meerkats can close their ears to keep out sand while they are digging.

Eating habits

Meerkats eat different types of food in different ways.

A meerkat picks up a snail and sucks its body out of its shell.

Before a meerkat can eat an egg, it has to crack it open.

A meerkat holds something big, such as a snake, in its paws. Then it tears off chunks.

This meerkat is
trying to eat
a scorpion.

Scorpions can be deadly when they sting
with their tails, so meerkats bite them off
first and then eat the body.

Keeping watch

When meerkats are above ground, eagles and jackals hunt them. Meerkats take turns to watch for danger.

This meerkat has climbed a bush to see what's nearby.

A meerkat that's keeping watch makes noises to tell things to its mob.

wuheep wuheep

Most of the time it squeaks to tell the others that they're safe.

HA WA HA WA

WOO YAP WOO YAP

It barks if it spots a dangerous animal on the ground.

If the danger is in the sky, it makes a different sound.

Action stations

Meerkats try to stay safe together.

When one meerkat spots danger, every member of the mob stops to look.

If dangerous animals or birds get too close, the meerkats scamper to their burrow.

They take cover in small holes when they're far from their burrow.

They stay under the ground until it's safe to come out again.

Meerkats sometimes hide when they see a plane in the sky.

Keep back!

Sometimes meerkats try to scare animals that attack them.

This meerkat is hissing.

It's telling other animals to stay away.

If a meerkat is very scared, it lies on its back and shows its teeth and claws.

Meerkats stay close together to frighten a dangerous snake.

They lift their tails so they look more scary too.

They keep scaring the snake until it slithers away.

Baby meerkats

Baby meerkats are called pups. Pups grow inside their mother for about 75 days.

When a mother is ready to have her pups, she goes inside the burrow.

Four or five pups are born. They can't see or hear yet and they don't have much fur.

The pups drink their mother's milk. It helps them to get bigger and stronger.

These pups are now three weeks old.
They have just left their burrow for
the first time.

Babysitters

A mother takes care of her pups with the help of other meerkats in the mob.

Another meerkat stays to protect the pups whenever their mother is hunting.

Adult meerkats also bring food to the burrow for the pups to eat.

Several adults help to carry the pups if they move to a new burrow.

Pups can drink milk
from other female
meerkats as well
as their mother.

These pups will
keep drinking
milk until
they're two
months old.

In training

Meerkat pups have lots to learn
as they grow up.

These pups are
finding out
ways to fight
as they play.

All the adult meerkats in
a mob teach the pups.

Pups watch adult meerkats
to learn how to look
out for danger.

They discover
where to dig for
food by following
adults too.

The adults also
show them how to
catch small animals
with their paws.

Angry mobs

Meerkat mobs try to stay apart. They use smells to mark where they live.

Meerkats mark trees or rocks with a smelly liquid.

They also leave piles of dung that has their smell.

Different mobs find out that meerkats already live here when they sniff the smells.

Sometimes mobs fight each other in fierce
battles. They fight with their teeth and claws.

These meerkats have
spotted another
mob nearby.

They're running and jumping
to chase the other mob away.

Meerkat messages

Meerkats use their bodies and make noises to tell each other things.

A big meerkat rubs its chin on smaller meerkats. This shows that it's in charge.

It barges into others with the side of its body to prove that it's strong.

eeee eeee

Pups squeak when they're lost until adult meerkats come to find them.

Meerkats purr and keep their tails high so they can find each other in tall grass.

Meerkats make at least 20 different types of sounds.

peep hooo   trill ga   haa grr whrr

Glossary

Here are some of the words in this book you might not know. This page tells you what they mean.

 mob - a group of meerkats. Meerkats live together in mobs.

 burrow - a hole or tunnel in the ground where some animals live.

 claw - a sharp nail. Meerkats have four claws on each of their paws.

 scorpion - a small animal with eight legs and a tail that it uses to sting.

 jackal - a type of wild dog. Jackals eat meerkats.

 pup - a baby meerkat. A mother has four or five pups at a time.

 mark - to leave a smell. Meerkats mark where they live.

Websites to visit

You can visit exciting websites to find out more about meerkats. For links to sites with video clips and activities, go to the Usborne Quicklinks website at **www.usborne.com/quicklinks** and type in the keywords "**beginners meerkats**".

Always ask an adult before using the internet and make sure you follow these basic rules:
1. Never give out personal information, such as your name, address, school or telephone number.
2. If a website asks you to type in your name or email address, check with an adult first.

The websites are regularly reviewed and the links at Usborne Quicklinks are updated. However, Usborne Publishing is not responsible and does not accept liability for the content or availability of any website other than its own. We recommend that children are supervised while on the internet.

This adult meerkat is taking its baby out of the burrow for the very first time.

Index

Acknowledgements

Photographic manipulation by John Russell

Photo credits

The publishers are grateful to the following for permission to reproduce material:
Cover © Nigel Dennis/Getty Images; **p1** © Robin Hoskyns/Biosphoto/FLPA; **p2-3** © Klein and Hubert/naturepl.com; **p4** © J.-L. Klein and M.-L. Hubert/FLPA; **p5** © Alexander von Duren/Tierfotoagentur/FLPA; **p7** © Sean Crane/Minden Pictures/FLPA; **p8** © Cavan Images/offset.com/photos/shutterstock; **p10** © Alain Mafart-Renodier/Biosphoto/FLPA; **p13** © BIOSPHOTO/Alamy Stock Photo; **p14** © Richard Du Toit/Minden Pictures/FLPA; **p16** © Roy Toft/Getty Images; **p18** © Riccardo_Cioli/thinkstock/Getty Images; **p21** © Will Burrard-Lucas/naturepl.com; **p23** © David & Micha Sheldon/Getty Images; **p24** © J.-L. Klein and M.-L. Hubert/FLPA; **p27** © J.-L. Klein and M.-L. Hubert/naturepl.com; **p29** © Sean Crane/Minden Pictures/FLPA; **p31** © Robin Hoskyns/Biosphoto/FLPA.